Sapna Malik

Malware Detection in Android Phones

Anchor Academic
Publishing

Malik, Sapna: Malware Detection in Android Phones, Hamburg, Anchor Academic Publishing 2017

Buch-ISBN: 978-3-96067-204-3
PDF-eBook-ISBN: 978-3-96067-704-8
Druck/Herstellung: Anchor Academic Publishing, Hamburg, 2017

Bibliografische Information der Deutschen Nationalbibliothek:
Die Deutsche Nationalbibliothek verzeichnet diese Publikation in der Deutschen Nationalbibliografie; detaillierte bibliografische Daten sind im Internet über http://dnb.d-nb.de abrufbar.

Bibliographical Information of the German National Library:
The German National Library lists this publication in the German National Bibliography. Detailed bibliographic data can be found at: http://dnb.d-nb.de

© Anchor Academic Publishing, Imprint der Diplomica Verlag GmbH
Hermannstal 119k, 22119 Hamburg
http://www.diplomica-verlag.de, Hamburg 2017
Printed in Germany

TABLE OF CONTENTS

CHAPTER 1: INTRODUCTION

The smartphone has rapidly become an extremely prevalent computing platform, with just over 115 million devices sold in the third quarter of 2011, a 15% increase over the 100 million devices sold in the first quarter of 2011, and a 111% increase over the 54 million devices sold in the first quarter of 2010 [1], [2]. Android in particular has seen even more impressive growth, with the devices sold in the third quarter of 2011 (60.5 million) almost triple the devices sold in the third quarter of 2010 (20.5 million), and an associated doubling of market share [2]. This popularity has not gone unnoticed by malware authors. Despite the rapid growth of the Android platform, there are already well-documented cases of Android malware, such as DroidDream, which was discovered in over 50 applications on the official Android market in March 2011 [3]. Furthermore, it is [3] found that Android's built-in security features are largely insufficient, and that even non malicious programs can (unintentionally) expose confidential information. A study of 204,040 Android applications conducted in 2011 found 211 malicious applications on the official Android market and alternative marketplaces.

The problem of using a machine learning-based classifier to detect malware presents the challenge: given an application, we must extract some sort of feature representation of the application. To address this problem, we extract a heterogeneous feature set, and process each feature independently using multiple kernels .We train a One-Class Support Vector Machine using the feature set we get to classify the application as a benign or malware accordingly.

Background

The number of malicious applications targeting the Android system has literally exploded in recent years. While the security community, well aware of this fact, has proposed several methods for detection of Android malware, most of these are based on permission and API usage or the identification of expert features. Unfortunately, many of these approaches are susceptible to instruction level obfuscation techniques. Previous research on classic desktop malware has shown that some high level characteristics of the code, such as function call graphs, can be used to and similarities between samples while being more robust against certain obfuscation strategies. However, the identification of similarities in graphs is a non-trivial problem whose complexity hinders the use of these features for malware detection. In our project we use a method for malware detection based on efficient embedding of function call graphs with an explicit feature map inspired by a linear-time graph kernel. In an evaluation with 181 malware samples our method, purely based on structural features, outperforms several related approaches and detects 69% of the malware with few false alarms, while also allowing to pin-point malicious code structures within Android applications. The project got us good results with a smaller database of the ours. If a platform with higher resources is given it will produce good results.

Malware Threats to Mobile Oss

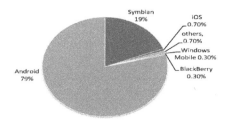

Figure 1. Growth trend of total Android suspicious samples [4]

WHY ANDROID IS INSECURE

A from the University of Cambridge put some hard numbers to Android's security failings. The conclusion finds that "on average 87.7% of Android devices are exposed to at least one of 11 known critical vulnerabilities."

Data for the study was collected through the group's "Device Analyzer" app, which has been available for free on the Play Store since May 2011. After the participants opted into the survey, the University says it collected daily Android version and build number information from over 20,400 devices. The study then compared this version information against 13 critical vulnerabilities (including the Stage fright vulnerabilities) dating back to 2010. Each individual device was then labelled "secure" or "insecure" based on whether or not its OS version was

4

patched against these vulnerabilities or placed in a special "maybe secure" category if it could have gotten a specialized, back ported fix.

The study found that Google's Nexus devices were the most secure out there, with a FUM score of 5.2 out of 10. Surprisingly, LG was next with 4.0, followed by Motorola, Samsung, Sony, and HTC, respectively.

With 87 % of devices flagged as insecure on any given day, the study really shows how far the Android ecosystem has to go to protect its users. Google and some OEMs have committed to a monthly security update program, but that is usually for devices that are less than two years old (Google recently bumped Nexus devices to three years) and only for flagship devices. The vast majority of Android sales are not flagship devices. Until Google re-architects Android to support centralized, device-agnostic updates, we just don't see a solution to Android's security problems.

Android Architecture

Android operating system is a stack of software components which is roughly divided into five sections and four main layers as shown below in the architecture diagram [5].

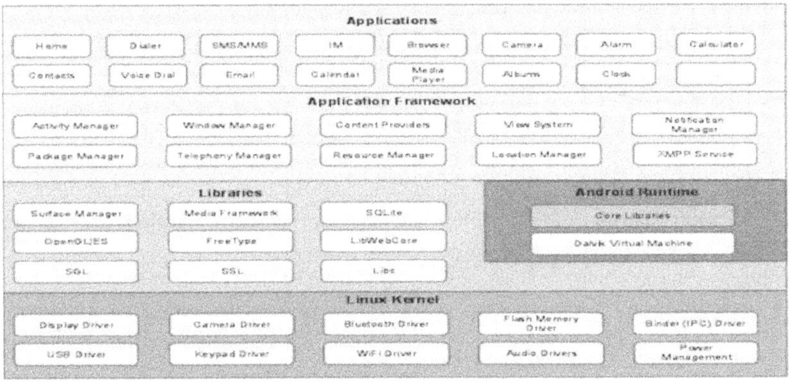

Figure 2. Android Architecture [5]

5

Linux kernel

At the bottom of the layers is Linux - Linux 3.6 with approximately 115 patches [5]. This provides a level of abstraction between the device hardware and it contains all the essential hardware drivers like camera, keypad, display etc. Also, the kernel handles all the things that Linux is really good at such as networking and a vast array of device drivers, which take the pain out of interfacing to peripheral hardware.

Libraries

On top of Linux kernel there is a set of libraries including open-source Web browser engine WebKit, well known library libc, SQLite database which is a useful repository for storage and sharing of application data, libraries to play and record audio and video, SSL libraries responsible for Internet security etc.

Android Libraries

This category encompasses those Java-based libraries that are specific to Android development. Examples of libraries in this category include the application framework libraries in addition to those that facilitate user interface building, graphics drawing and database access. A summary of some key core Android libraries available to the Android developer is as follows −

- **android.app** − Provides access to the application model and is the cornerstone of all Android applications.

- **android.content** − Facilitates content access, publishing and messaging between applications and application components.

- **android.database** − Used to access data published by content providers and includes SQLite database management classes.

- **android.opengl** − A Java interface to the OpenGL ES 3D graphics rendering API.

- **android.os** − Provides applications with access to standard operating system services including messages, system services and inter-process communication.

- **android.text** − Used to render and manipulate text on a device display.

- **android.view** – the fundamental building blocks of application user interfaces.

- **android.widget** – A rich collection of pre-built user interface components such as buttons, labels, list views, layout managers, radio buttons etc.

- **android.webkit** – A set of classes intended to allow web-browsing capabilities to be built into applications.

Having covered the Java-based core libraries in the Android runtime, it is now time to turn our attention to the C/C++ based libraries contained in this layer of the Android software stack.

Android Runtime

This is the third section of the architecture and available on the second layer from the bottom. This section provides a key component called **Dalvik Virtual Machine** which is a kind of Java Virtual Machine specially designed and optimized for Android.

The Dalvik VM makes use of Linux core features like memory management and multi-threading, which is intrinsic in the Java language. The Dalvik VM enables every Android application to run in its own process, with its own instance of the Dalvik virtual machine.

The Android runtime also provides a set of core libraries which enable Android application developers to write Android applications using standard Java programming language.

Application Framework

The Application Framework layer provides many higher-level services to applications in the form of Java classes. Application developers are allowed to make use of these services in their applications.

The Android framework includes the following key services –

- **Activity Manager** – Controls all aspects of the application lifecycle and activity stack.

- **Content Providers** – Allows applications to publish and share data with other applications.

- **Resource Manager** – Provides access to non-code embedded resources such as strings, color settings and user interface layouts.

- **Notifications Manager** – Allows applications to display alerts and notifications to the user.

- **View System** – An extensible set of views used to create application user interfaces.

Applications

You will find all the Android application at the top layer. You will write your application to be installed on this layer only. Examples of such applications are Contacts Books, Browser, Games etc.

Application components are the essential building blocks of an Android application. These components are loosely coupled by the application manifest file *AndroidManifest.xml* that describes each component of the application and how they interact.

There are following four main components that can be used within an Android application:

Components	Description
Activities	They dictate the UI and handle the user interaction to the smart phone screen
Services	They handle background processing associated with an application.
Broadcast Receivers	They handle communication between Android OS and applications.
Content Providers	They handle data and database management issues.

Additional Components

There are additional components which will be used in the construction of above mentioned entities, their logic, and wiring between them. These components are –

Components	Description
Fragments	Represents a portion of user interface in an Activity.
Views	UI elements that are drawn on-screen including buttons, lists forms etc.
Layouts	View hierarchies that control screen format and appearance of the views.
Intents	Messages wiring components together.
Resources	External elements, such as strings, constants and drawable pictures.
Manifest	Configuration file for the application.

Malware

- More serious malware threats
- Suspicious samples increasing rapidly

Fake Installer

Android.FakeInstaller is a widespread mobile malware family. It has spoofed the Olympic Games Results App, Skype, Flash Player, Opera and many other top applications. This is not news in the mobile malware world, the FakeInstaller family is one of the most prevalent malware that we have analysed. More than 60 % of Android samples processed by McAfee are FakeInstallers. This threat has become more dangerous, adding server-side polymorphism, obfuscation, antireversing techniques and frequent recompilation, all to avoid detection by antivirus solutions.

Android.FakeInstaller sends SMS messages to premium rate numbers, without the user's consent, passing itself off as the installer for a legitimate application. There are a large number of variants for this malware, and it is distributed on hundreds of websites and fake markets. The spread of this malware increases every day.

Figure 3. Icons of Android.FakeInstallers.

9

The deception starts when users search for a popular application and access a fake official site or fake market via search engines or social networks. Applications appear to be legitimate, including screenshots, descriptions, user reviews, videos, etc. Victims fall into the trap of downloading and installing the malware. When Android.FakeInstaller is executed, it displays a service agreement that tells the user that one or more SMS's will be sent; this agreement has been found in Russian or English.

The interface can be confusing. The user is forced to click an Agree or Next button, which sends the premium SMS messages. We have also seen versions that send the messages before the victim clicks a button.

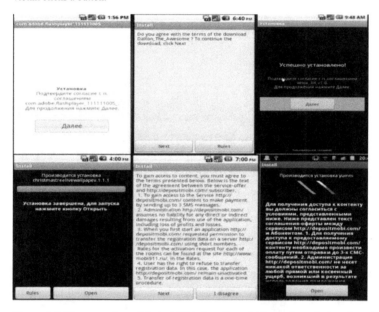

Figure 4. Different versions of Android.FakeInstaller, which simulates the install or download screen of a legitimate application.

After the button is pressed, FakeInstaller sometimes displays a fake download-progress bar. Finally, the dialog closes or redirects the browser to another fake market. Users will probably never get the application they want.

Polymorphic Server

In the wild we find several variants of FakeInstallers that have the main payload in common but have different code implementations. Some of them also have an extra payload. Generally each family is associated with a set of servers, domains, and fake applications markets.

This relationship is very strong because most FakeInstallers are server-side polymorphics, which means the server (according to its configuration) could provide different APK files for the same URL request.

When a victim requests an application from a fake market, the server redirects the browser to another server that processes the request and sends a customized APK which has an associated ID in the generated URL. The APK file is associated with the victim's IP address.

For example: Fake "Opera Mini 6.5" APK files were download from one URL (http://[censored]loads.ru/tds?r=3967) but accessed from two IP addresses (A and B). As a result, the browser gets redirected to different URLs and downloads very similar APK files that contain a few differences in the file res/raw/config.txt, which is related to the redirected URL.

The following image shows differences inside the file res/raw/config.txt, which is in samples downloaded from IP addresses A and B.

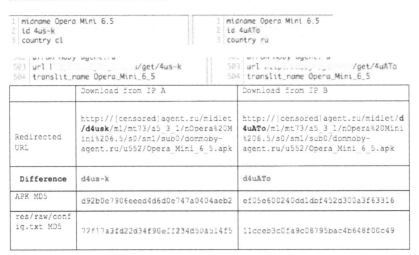

Figure 5. Format of Source file res/raw/config.txt

Consequently this modification produces changes in the digital signature (MANIFEST, MYKEY2.SF, and MYKEY2.RSA). In other variants this malware include an image (of a Russian joke) to increase or change the APK file size.

SMS Premium Rate Numbers

Previous versions of FakeInstaller were created only for Eastern European users, but malware developers have expanded their fraud to other countries–adding instructions to get the Mobile Country Code and Mobile Network Code of the device. Based on that information, Android/FakeInstaller selects the premium-rate numbers and the text for SMS messages.

The first versions of SMS message numbers were inside the DEX file, but in recent versions they come inside an encrypted XML file inside the APK, which depends on the server. We have found FakeInstaller samples that send up to seven premium SMS messages.

Avoiding Analysis: Java Obfuscation and Recompilation

Normally in one fake market all the applications include the same DEX file. After a while, the DEX file changes for all. Malware authors change their DEX files with newly recompiled obfuscated versions of the same code or implement new functions and include cosmetic changes, animations of fake installation progress bars, icons, texts, etc.

The most recent versions of FakeInstallers include different recompiled obfuscated versions of the same source code, changed source filenames, line numbers, field names, method names, argument names, variable names, etc.

In the following image we see two obfuscated versions of the same variant distributed in the same fake market on two days:

Figure 6. Variants of FakeInsatller

Obfuscators such as ProGuard or DexGuard can remove the debugging information and replace all names with meaningless character sequences, so it is much harder to reverse-engineer the code. Some versions, such as Android.FakeInstaller.S, also include antireversing techniques to avoid dynamic analysis and prevent the malware from running in an emulator.

Botnet Techniques

There are versions of Android.FakeInstaller that not only send SMS messages to premium rate numbers, but also include a backdoor to receive commands from a remote server. FakeInstaller.S uses "Android Cloud to Device Messaging" to register the infected devices in a database and send them messages (URLs) from malware authors Google accounts.

13

Distribution Techniques

Beside the server-side polymorphics we have to consider the daily creation of new fake websites and fake markets. These sites redirect the victim's downloads to a set of IP addresses and domains.

Some of these sites look fairly convincing and grab new victims easily because they are indexed in search engines like Yandex, which has a great position in the results ranking.

To avoid detections and appear more dependable, some fake sites redirect the application's download link from malicious to clean APK files, but after a while they restore the links.

We have also seen that fake-sites URLs are shared via Twitter by bot accounts and fake Facebook profiles:

Conclusion

Malware authors appear to make lots of money with this type of fraud, so they are determined to continue improving their infrastructure, code, and techniques to try to avoid antivirus software. It's an ongoing struggle, but we are constantly working to keep up with their advances.

CHAPTER 2: METHODOLOGY

Our method for the detection of Android malware is based on two key observations. First, malicious functionality of an Android application often concentrates on only a small number of its functions and second, similar malicious code is often found throughout the malware landscape as attackers reuse existing code to infect different applications.

Here, we are describing our approach of malware detection in android system. Following are the steps involved:

Step 1: Upload an android application file of .apk extension.

Step 2: Decompilation of the android application.

Step 3: The function call graph for the application is extracted, which contains a node for each function of the application. Nodes are labelled according to the instructions contained in their corresponding functions.

Step 4: Neighbourhood Hash Graph Kernel converts the function call graph input into a feature set which can be classified by the SVM (Support vector Machine).

Step 5: Support Vector Machine matches the function call graphs of the application with other malware applications to identify whether the application is malicious or not.

The project is divided into following three modules:-

REVERSE ENGINEERING OF THE ANDROID APPLICATION

In reverse engineering of the android application, we decompile the application into .java files so that methods along with their class names can be extracted. We used the decompiled code to draw a flow graph of any given android application. Following are the steps involved:

1. Conversion of .apk file to jar file

   Here, we use one application programming interface namely dex2jar. There is no direct method for getting java source code from the .apk file.

2. Conversion of jar file to java files

Here, we use one application programming interface namely jd-clid. This is a command line tool used for decompiling jar files into java files.

Dex

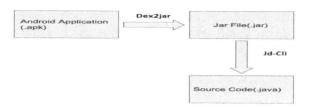

Figure 7. Steps of converting Dex to Jar file

FUNCTION CALL GRAPH CREATION

A call graph is a directed graph whose vertices, representing the functions a program is composed of, are interconnected through directed edges which symbolize function calls. Call graphs are generated from a binary executable through static analysis of the decompiled byte code.

To create the function call graph for the android application we have used **FlowDroid**framework.

FLOWDROID FEATURES

FLOWDROID, the first fully context, field, object and flow sensitive taint analysis which considers the Android application lifecycle and UI widgets, and which features a novel, particularly precise variant of an on-demand alias analysis;

A full open-source implementation of FLOWDROIDDROIDBENCH, a novel, open and comprehensive micro benchmark suite for Android flow analyses.

A set of experiments confirming superior precision and recall of FLOWDROID compared to the commercial tools AppScan Source and Fortify SCA.

16

A set of experiments applying FLOWDROID to over 500 apps from Google Play and about 1000 malware apps from the VirusShare project.

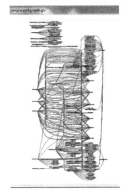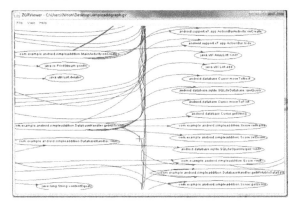

Figure 8. Function Call Graph

Labelling of Flow Graph

Nodes are labelled according to the instructions contained in their corresponding functions. In addition, nodes of the function call graph are labelled to characterize their content conveniently by short bit sequences. Intuitively, the extracted function call graphs are directed graphs containing a node for each of the application's functions and edges from callers to callees. Moreover, a labelled function call graph can be constructed by attaching a label to each node. Formally, this graph can be represented as a 4-tuple $G = (V, E, L, l)$, where V is a finite set of nodes and each node v belonging to V is associated with one of the application's functions. E is a subset of V XV denotes the set of directed edges, where an edge from a node v1 to a node v2 indicates a call from the function represented by v1 to the function represented by v2. Finally, L is the multiset of labels in the graph and $l: V \rightarrow L$ is a labelling function, which assigns a label to each node by considering properties of the function it represents. The design of the labelling function ` is crucial for the success of our method. While in principle, a unique label could be assigned to each node, this would not allow the method to exploit properties shared between functions. By contrast, a suitable labelling function maps two nodes onto the same label if their functions share properties relevant to the detection task. Moreover, labelling must be robust

17

against small changes in the code such as identifier renaming or branch inversion. To meet these requirements, we propose to label nodes according to the type of the instructions contained in their respective functions. Reviewing the Dalvik specification, we define 15 distinct categories of instructions based on their functionality as shown in Table 1. Each node can thus be labelled using a 15-bit field, where each bit is associated with one of the categories.

Category	Bit	Category	Bit
nop	1	branch	9
move	2	arrayop	10
return	3	instanceop	11
monitor	4	staticop	12
test	5	invoke	13
new	6	unop	14
throw	7	binop	15
jump	8		

Formally, the function ` can be defined as follows:

We denote the set of categories by C= {c1; c2; _ _ _; cm} and the function associated with a node v by f_v. The label l (v) of a node v $\in$ V is then a bit field of length m, i.e.

l(v) = [b_1(v), b_2(v) ; .... ; b_m(v)] where

$$b_c(v) = \begin{cases} 1 & \text{if } f_v \text{ contains an instruction from category } c \\ 0 & \text{otherwise.} \end{cases}$$

Consequently, the set of labels L is given by a subset of all possible 15-bit sequences.

CLASSIFICATION

Machine learning provides us with various algorithms for the classification problem the chief ones are:-

- Linear regression
- Logistic regression

- Nearest neighbour classifier

- Decision Trees

- Random Forests

- Neural network classifier

- Support vector machines (SVM)

Our project uses the Support Vector Machine to classify malicious and non-malicious applications. The brief explanation of the various algorithms is given below

LINEAR REGRESSION

Linear regression is a simple approach to supervised learning. It assumes that the dependence of Y on X1, X2, . . .Xp is linear. In simple linear regression using a single predictor X., we assume a model

$Y = \beta0 + \beta1X + \varepsilon$,

Where $\beta0$ and $\beta1$ are two unknown constants that represent the intercept and slope, also known as coefficients or parameters, and ε is the error term.

LOGISTIC REGRESSION

Logistic regression belongs to the family of classifiers known as the exponential or log-linear classifiers. Like naive Bayes, it work by log-linear classifier extracting some set of weighted features from the input, taking logs, and combining them linearly (meaning that each feature is multiplied by a weight and then added up). Technically, logistic regression refers to a classifier that classifies an observation into one of two classes, and multinomial logistic regression is used when classifying into more than two classes. The most important difference between naive Bayes and logistic regression is that logistic regression is a discriminative classifier while naive Bayes is a generative classifier.

NEAREST NEIGHBOR CLASSIFIER

Nearest neighbourhood or 1-nearest neighbourhood doesn't perform satisfactorily in most cases, because it is too sensitive to the noise of the single nearest neighbouring data point. K-nearestneighbourhood performs quite well in many domains. But notice that it does not recognize the "boundary" of the different patterns. Besides, k-nearest neighbourhood may be influenced by the density of the neighbouring data points along the border. In the following diagram, intuitively the output of the query (the dark triangle) should be a cross, because it is on the cross side. However, k-nearest neighbourhood's conclusion tends to be a circle, because among the k nearest neighbouring data points, the majority are circles.

DECISION TREES

The idea of a decision tree is to partition the input space into small segments, and label these small segments with one of the various output categories. However, conventional decision tree only does the partitioning to the coordinate axes. It is plausible that with the growth of the tree, the input space can be partitioned into tiny segments so as to recognize subtle patterns. However, overgrown trees lead to overfitting.

RANDOM FORESTS

Random Forests grows many classification trees. To classify a new object from an input vector, put the input vector down each of the trees in the forest. Each tree gives a classification, and we say the tree "votes" for that class. The forest chooses the classification having the most votes (over all the trees in the forest).

Each tree is grown as follows:

1. If the number of cases in the training set is N, sample N cases at random - but with replacement, from the original data. This sample will be the training set for growing the tree.

2. If there are M input variables, a number m<<M is specified such that at each node, m variables are selected at random out of the M and the best split on these m is used to split the node. The value of m is held constant during the forest growing.

3. Each tree is grown to the largest extent possible. There is no pruning.

The forest error rate depends on two things:

- The correlation between any two trees in the forest. Increasing the correlation increases the forest error rate.

- The strength of each individual tree in the forest. A tree with a low error rate is a strong classifier. Increasing the strength of the individual trees decreases the forest error rate.

Reducing m reduces both the correlation and the strength. Increasing it increases both. Somewhere in between is an "optimal" range of m - usually quite wide. Using the oob error rate (see below) a value of m in the range can quickly be found. This is the only adjustable parameter to which random forests is somewhat sensitive.

NEURAL NETWORK CLASSIFIER

To mimic the working of a human brain artificial neural networks are developed, they are meant to function like the neural networks in the brain. The neural network uses the examples to automatically infer rules for recognizing handwritten digits. Furthermore, by increasing the number of training examples, the network can learn more about handwriting, and so improve its accuracy.

"A computing system made up of a number of simple, highly interconnected processing elements, which process information by their dynamic state response to external inputs."

How Neural Networks Learn

Artificial neural networks (ANNs) typically start out with randomized weights for all their neurons. This means that they don't "know" anything and must be trained to solve the particular problem for which they are intended. Broadly speaking, there are two methods for training an ANN, depending on the problem it must solve.

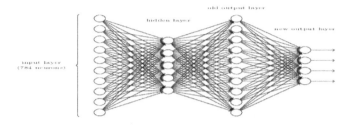

Figure 9. Neural Network Primer [6]

A self-organizing ANN (often called a Kohonen after its inventor) is exposed to large amounts of data and tends to discover patterns and relationships in that data. Researchers often use this type to analyse experimental data.

A back-propagation ANN, conversely, is trained by humans to perform specific tasks. During the training period, the teacher evaluates whether the ANN's output is correct. If it's correct, the neural weightings that produced that output are reinforced; if the output is incorrect, those weightings responsible are diminished. This type is most often used for cognitive research and for problem-solving applications.

Implemented on a single computer, an artificial neural network is typically slower than a more traditional algorithmic solution. The ANN's parallel nature, however, allows it to be built using multiple processors, giving it a great speed advantage at very little development cost. The parallel architecture also allows ANNs to process very large amounts of data very efficiently. When dealing with large, continuous streams of information, such as speech recognition or machine sensor data, ANNs can operate considerably faster than their linear counterparts.

Artificial neural networks have proved useful in a variety of real-world applications that deal with complex, often incomplete data. The first of these were in visual pattern recognition and speech recognition. In addition, recent programs for text-to-speech have utilized ANNs. Many handwriting analysis programs (such as those used in popular PDAs) are powered by ANNs.

Automated and robotic factories are now being monitored by ANNs that control machinery, adjust temperature settings, and diagnose malfunctions and more. These ANNs can augment or replace skilled labour, making it possible for fewer people to do more work.

SUPPORT VECTOR MACHINE

SVM is responsible for finding a hyper plane that will differentiate between positive and negative examples' the goal is to separate the two classes by a function which is induced from available examples. The goal is to produce a classifier that will work well on unseen examples, i.e. it generalises well. Consider the example in Figure. Here there are many possible linear classifiers that can separate the data, but there is only one that maximises the margin (maximises the distance between it and the nearest data point of each class). This linear classifier is termed the optimal separating hyper plane. Intuitively, we would expect this boundary to generalise well as opposed to the other possible boundaries.

Figure 10. Optimal Separating Hyper plane

But one of the problems in this is that the dataset may not be linear enough to find a hyper plane for the data as shown in fig 6. So one needs to use a kernel function which will transform the input to a high dimensional implementation and convert the inputs into linearly separable data. As shown in fig 7.

23

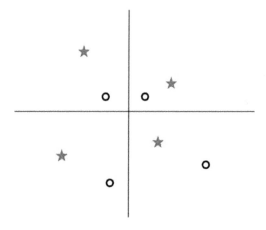

Figure 11. The data is linearly inseparable and so no hyper plane possible which will differentiate between the two examples.

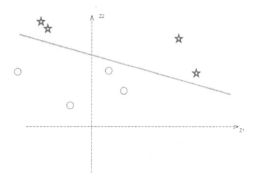

Figure 12. After applying kernel which transforms the input into another high dimensional space where the data is linearly separable.

There are various kernels that can be used to make this transformation as per the data the most well-known SVM kernels are Gaussian kernel, polynomial kernel etc. Our project uses Neighbourhood Hash Graph Kernel (NHGK) in the SVM.

Neighbourhood Hash Graph Kernel

The NHGK is a so called decomposition kernel as designed by Haussler [19]. As such, it is a kernel operating over an enumerable set of sub graphs in a labelled graph. It has low computational complexity and high expressiveness of the graph structure, but its main advantage is that it is able to run in time linear in the number of nodes and can therefore process graphs with thousands of nodes such as the function call graphs of Android applications. The main idea behind the NHGK is to condense the information contained in a neighbourhood into a single hash value.

This value is calculated over the labels of a neighbourhood and represents the distribution of the labels around a central node. It thus allows us to enumerate all neighbourhood sub graphs in linear time without running an isomorphism test over all pairs of neighbourhoods.

WHY SVM

All classification techniques have advantages and disadvantages, which are more or less important according to the data which are being analysed, and thus have a relative relevance. SVMs can be a useful tool for insolvency analysis, in the case of non-regularity in the data, for example when the data are not regularly distributed or have an unknown distribution. It can help evaluate information, i.e. financial ratios which should be transformed prior to entering the score of classical classification techniques. The advantages of the SVM technique can be summarised as follows:

1. By introducing the kernel, SVMs gain flexibility in the choice of the form of the threshold separating solvent from insolvent companies, which needs not be linear and even needs not have the same functional form for all data, since its function is non-parametric and operates locally. As a consequence they can work with financial ratios, which show a non-monotone relation to the score and to the probability of default, or which are non-linearly dependent and this without needing any specific work on each non-monotone variable.

2. Since the kernel implicitly contains a non-linear transformation, no assumptions about the functional form of the transformation, which makes data linearly separable, is necessary. The

transformation occurs implicitly on a robust theoretical basis and human expertise judgement beforehand is not needed.

3. SVMs provide a good out-of-sample generalization, if the parameters C and r (in the case of a Gaussian kernel) are appropriately chosen. This means that, by choosing an appropriate generalization grade, SVMs can be robust, even when the training sample has some bias.

4. SVMs deliver a unique solution, since the optimality problem is convex. This is an advantage compared to Neural Networks, which have multiple solutions associated with local minima and for this reason may not be robust over different samples.

5. With the choice of an appropriate kernel, such as the Gaussian kernel, one can put more stress on the similarity between companies, because the more similar the financial structure of two companies is, the higher is the value of the kernel. Thus when classifying a new company, the values of its financial ratios are compared with the ones of the support vectors of the training sample which is more similar to this new company. This company is then classified according to with which group it has the greatest similarity.

CHAPTER 3: VISUAL REPRESENTATION

Level-0 DFD

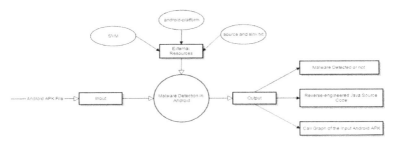

Figure 13. Level 0 DFD

Basic Program Structure

Figure 14. Program Structure

CHAPTER 4: DEVELOPMENT PHASES

We are provided with a dataset of 91 android applications out of which roughly 70% are We are provided with a dataset of 91 android applications out of which roughly 70% are malware while 30% are benign. Our project was mainly divided into 3 main phases

Preprocessing of dataset

In this phase we pre-process the data by following the following steps

- Decompiling of the application to get its source code

- Creation of function call graph

- Labelling of each node with a 15 bit number

- After pre-processing of the application we store the pre-processed data in a text file.

Analysis of dataset

After pre-processing we create a default vector corresponding to our malwares. This vector corresponds to the centroid of our dataset.

This default vector is used to compare the application under scrutiny to the degree of the malware in them. Our entire concept is based on the fact that each type of malware has similar structure.

After analysing the dataset we come to the conclusion that max hash value is 998 and the maximum frequency of the hash function is 775. These two facts help us reducing the size of the feature vector to a constant size of 775*998.

Classification

After creating the labels of the function of all the applications in the dataset. The dataset has been used for the training of the SVM. To train the SVM we have used NHGK kernel to map the data in the linearly separable dimensions. The advantage of NHGK kernel is that it reduces the graph isomorphism complexity to O (n). We store the processed hashed data of all the applications in a text file.

Result

We have successfully classified the android applications for fake installer malware. Our project can classify with an accuracy of 69%.

CHAPTER 5: APIs USED

Java assist

Javassist (Java Programming Assistant) makes Java bytecode manipulation simple. It is a class library for editing bytecodes in Java; it enables Java programs to define a new class at runtime and to modify a class file when the JVM loads it. Unlike other similar bytecode editors, Javassist provides two levels of API: source level and bytecode level. If the users use the source-level API, they can edit a class file without knowledge of the specifications of the Java bytecode. The whole API is designed with only the vocabulary of the Java language. You can even specify inserted bytecode in the form of source text; Javassist compiles it on the fly. On the other hand, the bytecode-level API allows the users to directly edit a class file as other editors.

Javassist can be used for the following:

- For specifying the bytecode using source code – can compile a fragment of source text online (e.g., just a single statement)

- For aspect-oriented programming (AOP) – can introduce new methods into a class and insert before/after/around advice at both the caller and callee sides

- For reflection at runtime – can use a metaobject that controls method calls on base-level objects

- For remote method invocation – can call a method on a remote object running on a web server, an alternative to Java RMI that does not need a stub compiler such as `rmic`

Soot

Soot is a Java optimization framework. It provides four intermediate representations for analysing and transforming Java bytecode:

- Baf: a streamlined representation of bytecode which is simple to manipulate.

- Jimple: a typed 3-address intermediate representation suitable for optimization.

- Shimple: an SSA variation of Jimple.

- Grimp: an aggregated version of Jimple suitable for decompilation and code inspection.

What input formats does Soot provide?

Currently, Soot can process code from the following sources:

- Java (bytecode and source code up to Java 7), including other languages that compile to Java bytecode, e.g. Scala

- Android bytecode

- Jimple intermediate representation (see below)

- Jasmin, a low-level intermediate representation.

What output formats does Soot provide?

Soot can produce (possibly transformed/instrumented/optimized) code in these output formats:

- Java bytecode

- Android bytecode

- Jimple

- Jasmin

Soot can go from any input format to any output format, i.e., for instance, allows the translation from Android to Java or Java to Jasmin.

dex2jar

dex2jar contains following component :

- dex-reader is designed to read the Dalvik Executable (.dex/.odex) format. It has a light weight API similar with ASM.

- dex-translator is designed to do the convert job. It reads the dex instruction to dex-ir format, after some optimize, convert to ASM format.

- dex-ir used by dex-translator, is designed to represent the dex instruction dex-tools tools to work with .class files.

- d2j-smali disassemble dex to smali files and assemble dex from smali files. different implementation to smali/baksmali, same syntax, but we support escape in type desc "Lcom/dex2jar\t\u1234;"

- dex-writer write dex same way as dex-reader.

jd-cli

jd-cmd is a command line Java Decompiler which uses JD Core from Java Decompiler project.

JADX

It targets dex directly, rather than java class bytecode, so it doesn't rely on dex2jar. i'm pleased by it's performance so far, and it's worth checking out:https://github.com/skylot/jadx

- it's mostly a cli, with a simple, "experimental" gui.

- it takes dex or jar files as input

- it can make a control flow graph.

- output is configurable -- you can chose to have "simple" branching, where it wont try to be smart about how it decompiles conditionals and loops. this can actually be much easier to read than jd-gui's pervasive "while(true) //a bunch of stuff" constructs.

FlowDroid

FlowDroid is a *context-, flow-, field-, object-sensitive and lifecycle-aware* static taint analysis tool for Android applications. Unlike many other static-analysis approaches for Android we aim for an analysis with very high recall and precision. To achieve this goal we had to accomplish two main challenges: To increase precision we needed to build an analysis that is context-, flow-, field- and object-sensitive; to increase recall we had to create a complete model of Android's app lifecycle.

Our analysis is based on Soot and Heros. FlowDroid uses a very precise callgraph which helps us to ensure flow- and context-sensitivity. Its IFDS-based flow functions guarantee field- and object-sensitivity. Because an accurate and efficient alias search is crucial for context-sensitivity in conjuction with field-sensitivity, we want to highlight this part of our analysis, which is inspired by Andromeda. The following code example shows how our approach tracks aliases:

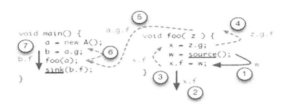

Figure 15. Approach for tracking Aliases [7]

We want to analyse if there is a connection from source to the sink. We start with the first line of the main method and analyse each statement successively. Note that in (3) a taint is assigned to a field (x.f) which starts a backward analysis. Now the statements are examined in the reverse order and we learn that z.g.f, a.g.f and b.f are aliases of x.f. The sink method takes b.f as input parameter, so there is a source-to-sink connection.

Furthermore, FlowDroid needs a complete modelling of Android's lifecycles and callbacks. Because sources and sinks for Android are provided by SuSi, we only have to look for entry points. Along with necessary meta information they are extracted from Android's manifest file, dex files and layout xml files. The latter allow us to consider user interaction callbacks defined in XML (for example button clicks) and discover additional sources in terms of password fields. Because user interaction cannot be predicted statically, FlowDroid generates a special main method which considers all possible combinations to make sure no taint is lost.

FlowDroid achieves 93% recall and 86% precision on DroidBench, our own Android benchmark suite. Despite its high precision FlowDroid is still capable of analyzing real-world applications and also performs well on SecuriBench Micro, a testsuite originally designed for web applications.

33

CHAPTER 6: SCREENSHOTS

The various windows that our project has used are:-

Basic UI

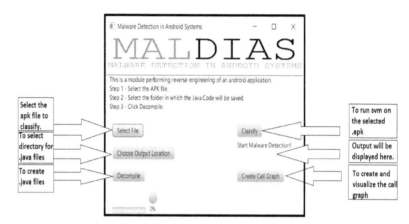

Figure 16. Description of Basic UI

FileSelector

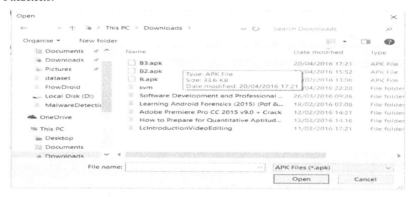

Figure 17. Selecting the application to classify

Application Decompiling

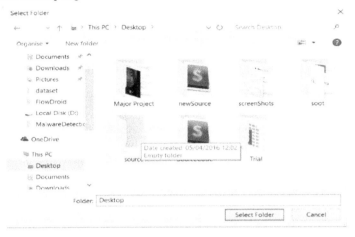

Figure 18. Selecting a Folder

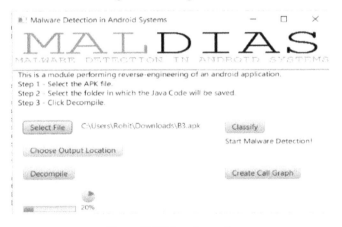

Figure 19. Click on decompile

Call graph generation

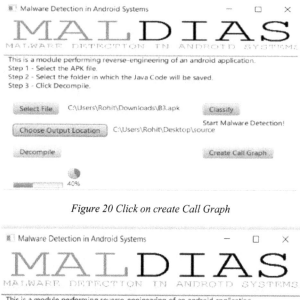

Figure 20 Click on create Call Graph

Figure 21. After Reverse Engineering

36

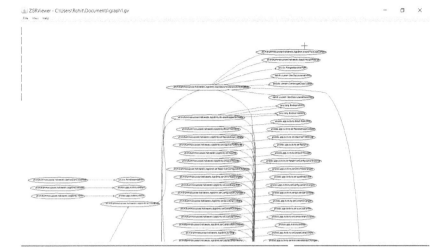

Figure 22. Call Graph of an application

Classification of malware

Figure 23. Classify the Application

CHAPTER 7: THE MAIN SOURCE CODE

The main java files that are used in the project, and their function are :-

CallGraphExample.java

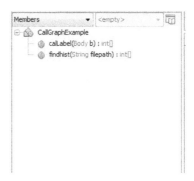

Figure 24. Snapshot of CallGraphExample.java

This java file is responsible for creating the function call graph .It takes the main .apk file of the application to classify and then also add the label for each and every function node.

MalwareDetectionAndroid.java

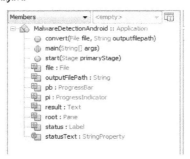

Figure 25. Snapshot of MalwareDetectionAndroid.java

This java file is the main class file of the project.It is responsible for the main GUI of the project.

Classifier.java

Figure 26. Snapshot of Classifier.java

This is the classification java file. Here the main Support Vector machine has been implemented. This makes use of already trained weight values and the default vector for a centroid of the malware programs.

Kernel.java

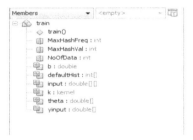

Figure 27. Snapshot of Kernel.java

This is the implementation of the main kernel Neighbourhood hash Graph Kernel. This converts the dataset into linearly seperable data.

Train.java

Figure 28. Snapshot of Train.java

This is used for the training of the SVM. This makes use of initially random weights then, it trains using 94 applications.

CHAPTER 8: CONCLUSION

In this work, we have presented a learning-based method for the detection of malicious Android applications. Our method employs an explicit feature map inspired by the neighbourhood hash graph kernel to represent applications based on their function call graphs. This representation is shown to be both, efficient and effective, for training an SVM that ultimately enables us to automaticallyidentify Android malware with a detection rate of 89% with 1% false positives, corresponding to one false alarm in 100 installed applications on a smartphone. As the vast majority of mobile malware targets the Android platform, this work focuses on Android malware detection. However, the method presented can be adapted to other platforms with minor changes, given that (a) function call graphs can be extracted and (b) instructions can be suitably categorized. Adapting the method to other platforms, including desktop systems, May thus be an interesting direction for future work. Moreover, combining existing classifiers based on contextual features with our structural detection approach seems promising.

REFERENCES

[1]   C. Kolbitsch, P. Comparetti, C. Kruegel, E. Kirda, X. Zhou, and X. Wang. E_ective and efficient malware detection at the end host. In Proc. of USENIX Security Symposium, 2009.

[2]   Android Malware Family Origins. Available at : https://www.fireeye.com/blog/threat-research/2016/03/android-malware-family-origins.html

[3]   Lookout Mobile Security. Security alert: Droiddream malware found in official android market.http://blog.mylookout.com/blog/2011/03/01/security-alert-malware-found-in-official-android-market-droiddream/

[4]   Jaiojaio Fu. Detecting & Preventing Privilege–Escalation on Android. Available at:http://slideplayer.com/slide/6624813/

[5]   Android Architecture. Available at : https://www.tutorialspoint.com/android/android_architecture.htm

[6]   Neural Network Primer: Part I" by Maureen Caudill, AI Expert, Feb. 1989

[7]   Alias Flow Available at : http://blogs.uni-paderborn.de/sse/files/2013/05/aliasFlow.png

[8]   Structural Detection of Android Malware using Embedded Call Graphs by Hugo Gascony, Fabian Yamaguchi Daniel Arp and Konrad Rieck University of Göttingen Göttingen, Germany.

[9]   X. Hu, T.-c. Chiueh, and K. G. Shin. Large-scale malware indexing using function-call graphs. In Proc. of the ACM conference on Computer and communications security, 2009.

[10]   V. Rastogi, Y. Chen, and X. Jiang. DroidChameleon: evaluating Android anti-malware against transformation attacks. In ASIACCS, pages 329–334. ACM, 2013.

[11]   Yajin Zhou, Zhi Wang, Wu Zhou, and Xuxian Jiang. Hey, you, get off of my market: Detecting malicious apps in official and alternative android markets. In Proceedings of the 19th Network and Distributed System Security Symposium, 2012.

[12]   William Enck, Damien Octeau, Patrick McDaniel, and Swarat Chaudhuri. A study of android application security. In Proceedings of the 20th USENIX Security Symposium, 2011.

www.ingramcontent.com/pod-product-compliance
Lightning Source LLC
La Vergne TN
LVHW052316060326
832902LV00021B/3933